Gemma

Insects

Anita Ganeri

Watts Books
London • New York • Sydney

© 1994 Watts Books

Watts Books
96 Leonard Street
London EC2A 4RH

Franklin Watts Australia
14 Mars Road
Lane Cove
NSW 2066

UK ISBN: 0 7496 1590 7

10 9 8 7 6 5 4 3 2 1

Dewey Decimal Classification 595.7

Series editor: Pippa Pollard
Editor: Jane Walker
Design: Visual Image
Artwork: Mainline Design
Cover artwork: Mainline Design
Photo research: Alison Renwick
Fact checking: Simone K. Lefolii

A CIP catalogue record for this book
is available from the British Library

Printed in Italy by
G. Canale & C. SpA

Contents

What is an insect?

Do you know the difference between an ant and a spider? An ant is an insect and a spider is not! You can tell this by counting the number of legs of each creature. An insect is an animal with six legs. Its body is divided into three parts – the head (top), the **thorax** (middle) and the **abdomen** (bottom). It has a hard coat around its body to protect it from being harmed.

▽ Look carefully at this hoverfly. Can you see its insect features?

Sizes and shapes

There are millions of different types of insect. In fact, there are more types of insect than of all other animals. Insects are usually quite small. They have to get rid of their hard coats in order to grow larger. But insects come in many shapes and colours. The five main insect groups are butterflies and moths; ants, wasps and bees; beetles; bugs; and flies.

▷ Ladybirds are easy to spot with their bright red and black coats.

▽ The rhinoceros beetle is one of the biggest insects. Its name is because of its long horn.

◁ Stick insects are the longest kind of insect. Some can measure over 33 centimetres.

◁ Dragonflies have long, thin bodies and long wings.

5

Insects of the world

Insects live all over the world. They quickly get used to different places and can survive by eating very little food. Insects live in deserts, in the polar regions, up mountains, in fields and gardens and even in people's homes. They can live in water and on dry land. Some have special features which help them to survive in difficult conditions.

▷ Caterpillars of the clothes moth live and feed on cotton and woollen clothes.

◁ The morpho butterfly lives in the rainforests of South America.

▷ The fog-drinking beetle lives in the dry desert. It drinks water that is trapped in fog.

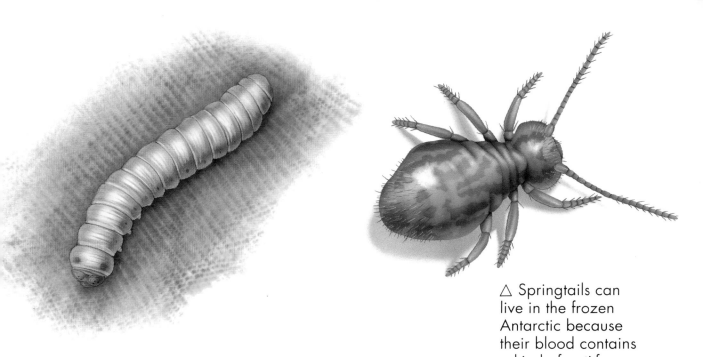

△ Springtails can live in the frozen Antarctic because their blood contains a kind of anti-freeze.

Nests and hives

Many insects do not have fixed homes. Some make nests and lay their eggs in them, to keep the eggs safe. But the adult insects do not live in these nests. Some insects, such as bees and ants, live in large groups and have special homes. Ants build nests on the ground or up in trees. Bees live in nests or in man-made **hives**.

▷ Tiny termites build nests out of mud and spit. Some nests are more than three times taller than an adult human.

▽ Bees build their honeycombs out of wax that is made inside their bodies.

△ A potter wasp makes its jar-shaped nest out of soft mud.

8

Finding a mate

Each year, most adult insects look for
a mate so that they can make eggs.
These will hatch into young insects.
Insects usually mate in spring when the
weather is warm. Male insects may use
lights, colours or even songs to
attract females. Some have to fight
off other males.

▽ Fireflies flash their
lights to get each
other's attention.

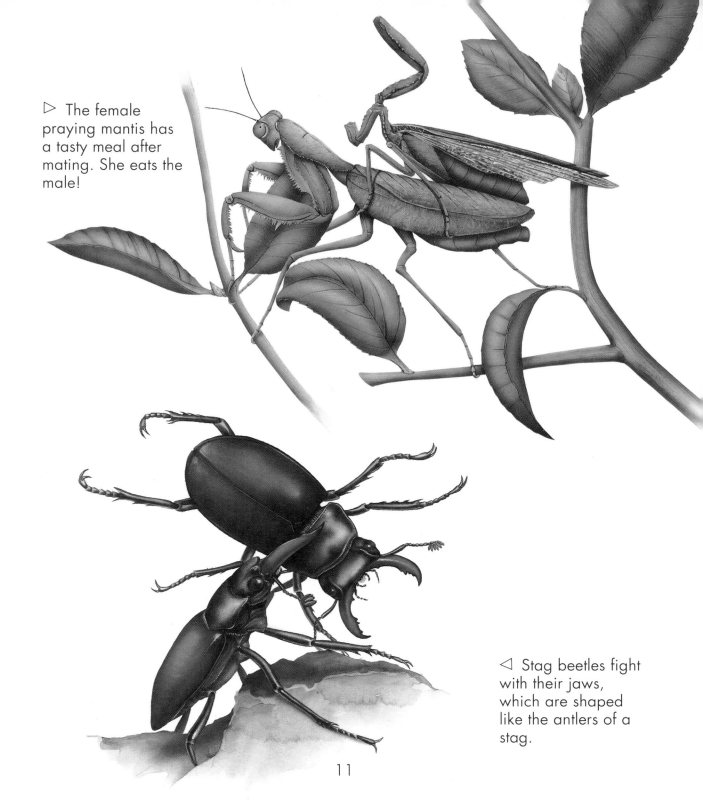

▷ The female praying mantis has a tasty meal after mating. She eats the male!

◁ Stag beetles fight with their jaws, which are shaped like the antlers of a stag.

11

Laying eggs

The females of many insects, such as wasps, ants and some moths, lay their eggs without finding a mate first. The eggs are small but tough. Insects lay their eggs on leaves, on stems, underground, in the bodies of other animals, in wood and in water. Some look for places which are safe, and where there is food for their young.

▷ The male giant water bug carries the eggs on his back until they hatch.

▽ Most insects lay their eggs and then leave them. But mother earwigs guard their eggs closely.

△ Horntails drill holes in plants with a long sharp part attached to their abdomen. They lay their eggs in these holes.

Time for a change

When young insects hatch out of their eggs, most look nothing like adult insects. Their bodies change as they grow up. For a butterfly, this happens in four steps – the egg, the **larva**, the **pupa** and the adult. A caterpillar is the larva of a butterfly. Here you can see how a butterfly grows from an egg into an adult insect.

▽ **2** The caterpillar eats leaves and grows. It grows a new skin each time it gets bigger.

▽ **1** The caterpillar (larva) hatches from its egg.

▷ This monarch butterfly has just emerged from its pupa case.

14

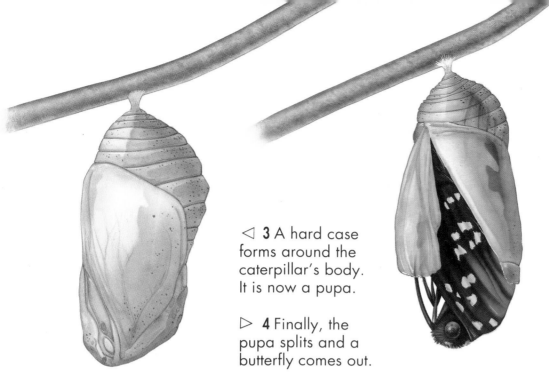

◁ **3** A hard case forms around the caterpillar's body. It is now a pupa.

▷ **4** Finally, the pupa splits and a butterfly comes out.

More changes

Like butterflies, grasshoppers begin life as eggs. But when they hatch, they look like little adults. They have to grow bigger until they reach full adult size. As they grow, they become too big for their old coats. These split and fall off, and the young grasshoppers grow bigger coats. This happens several times. They also grow wings.

▽ This grasshopper is pulling itself free from its old coat which is too small.

▷ **1** Dragonflies often lay their eggs in water.

▽ **2** The dragonfly larva, called a nymph, lives underwater. Nymphs are fierce hunters.

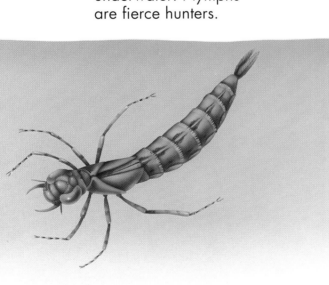

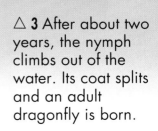

△ **3** After about two years, the nymph climbs out of the water. Its coat splits and an adult dragonfly is born.

17

Insect food

Insects eat all sorts of food. Many eat plants. Look for nibbled leaves in your garden. Bees and butterflies feed on **nectar** and **pollen** from flowers. Bugs suck juicy **sap** from plant stems. Meat-eating insects feed on dead animals as well as living ones. More unusual meals for insects include wooden furniture, clothes and even human blood.

▷ Butterflies suck up nectar through a long, hollow tube.

▽ Some honeypot ants store honey in their bodies. They squirt the honey out for other ants to eat.

△ Ground beetles use their big jaws like scissors to cut up grubs to eat.

18

Flying about

Many adult insects have wings and can fly from place to place. Flying is very useful. Insects can fly to find food and to escape from danger. Most insects have two pairs of wings. In some insects, the pairs of wings are joined together by tiny hooks so that they move together in the air. This makes it easier for the insect to fly. Some insects, such as flies, have only one pair of wings.

▷ Most insects do not fly very far. But millions of monarch butterflies fly 3,000 kilometres every year from Canada and the USA to Mexico.

▽ Butterfly wings are covered in tiny scales. These overlap, like tiles on the roof of a house.

▽ Dragonflies are superb fliers. They can dart and hover in the air as they chase other insects to eat.

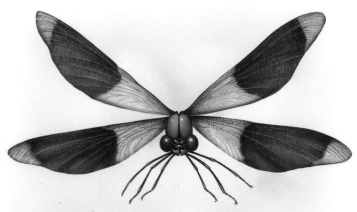

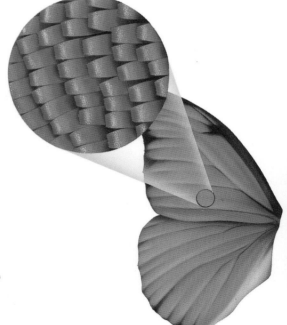

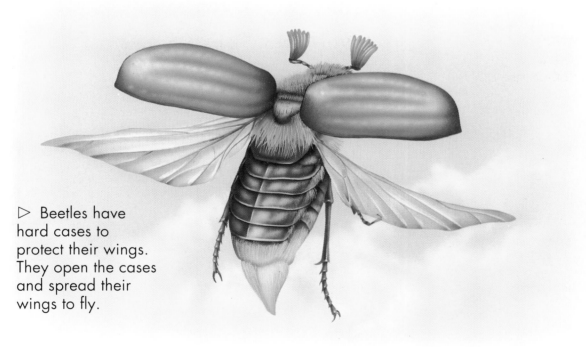

▷ Beetles have
hard cases to
protect their wings.
They open the cases
and spread their
wings to fly.

More ways of moving

A few insects, for instance most ants, as well as young insects cannot fly. Ants scurry about on their long, thin legs. Other insects, such as grasshoppers and fleas, use their long legs for jumping. Insects that live in water are often good swimmers. They use their legs as oars to paddle through the water.

▷ Some flies have sticky pads on their feet. This is how they can walk upside down on the ceiling.

▽ Pondskaters walk on the surface of the pond. They spread out their long legs so they do not sink.

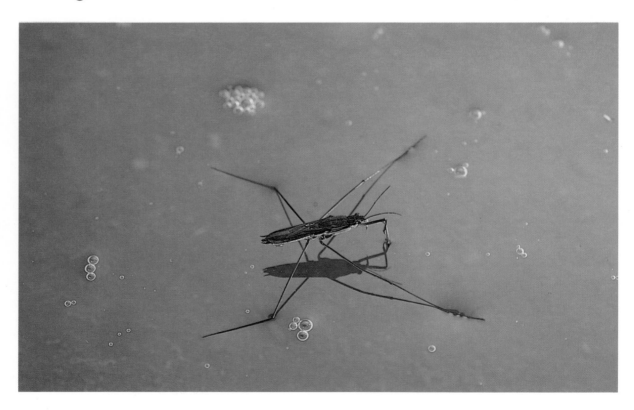

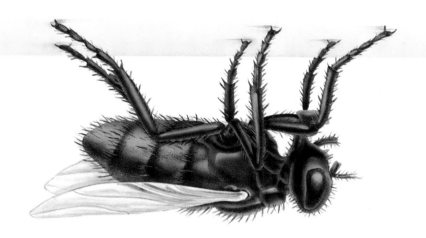

▽ Fleas can jump very high indeed. They can leap about 150 times their own height!

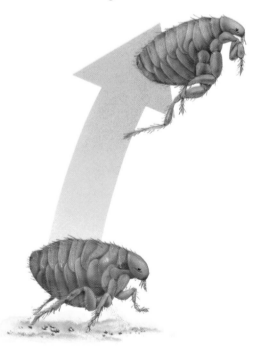

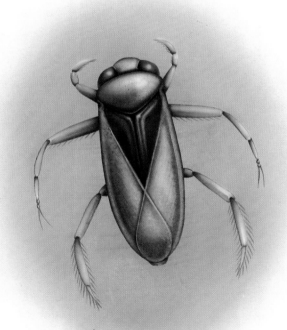

△ The water boatman swims on its back. It uses its legs as oars.

Seeing sense

No one knows exactly what an insect sees when it looks at the world around it. It probably does not see the same picture as we do. Insects' eyes are very different to our eyes. Many adult insects have three tiny simple eyes which may see shades of light and dark. They also have large **compound** eyes. These may be made of hundreds of tiny **lenses**.

▷ Bees can see special markings on flowers which we cannot see. The markings guide them to the flower's nectar.

▽ The male diopsid fly has very strange eyes on the end of stalks.

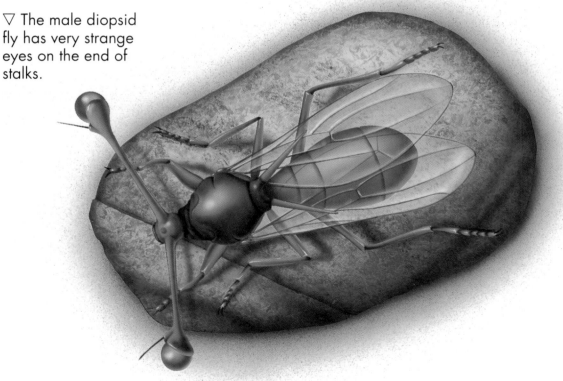

▽ A dragonfly's compound eyes are good for spotting food in the air.

Other senses

Insects do not have noses, tongues and fingers like you. But they can still smell, taste and feel things. Insects use their **antennae** for smelling and feeling, and some use them for tasting. They can also feel things with the hairs on their bodies. Insects use smells to find mates, to keep in contact with each other and to find food. So their antennae are very important.

▷ Some caterpillars are very hairy. The hairs react to sounds and make the caterpillars curl up, to protect themselves.

▽ Cockchafer beetles spread out their antennae like fans.

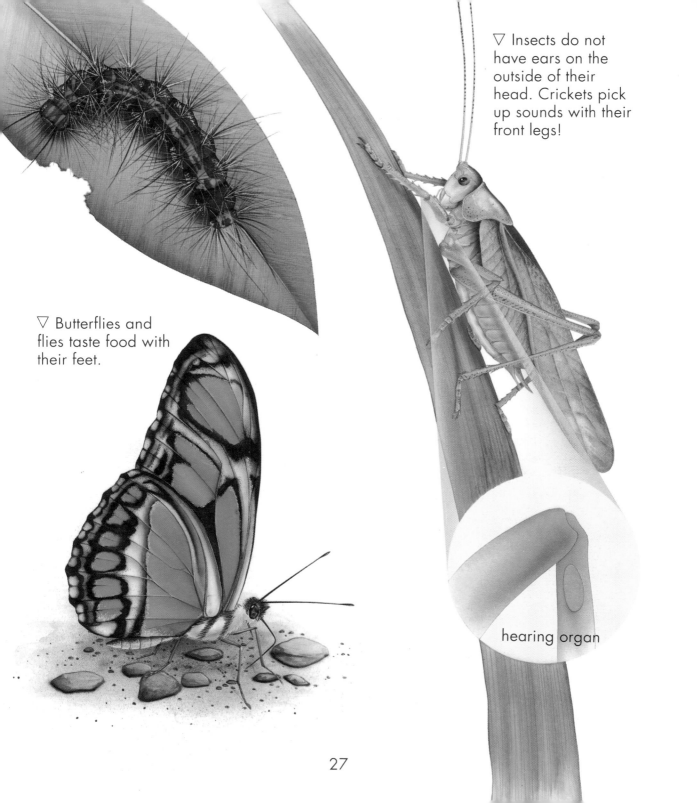

▽ Insects do not have ears on the outside of their head. Crickets pick up sounds with their front legs!

▽ Butterflies and flies taste food with their feet.

hearing organ

How do insects survive?

Many animals, such as birds and fish, feed on insects and their young. Insects have many ways of escaping from being eaten. Some fly or run away. Others sting or bite. Some use bright colours to warn their enemies not to attack. Others use their colours and shapes as disguises, to hide their bodies from view.

▷ This orchid mantis is perfectly disguised.

▷ The eye patterns on the peacock butterfly's wings are used to scare away hungry birds.

▽ Bombardier beetles squirt a jet of hot gas at their attackers.

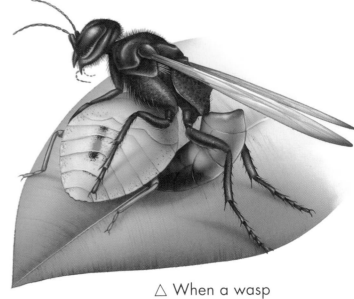

△ When a wasp stings, it injects a small amount of poison into its victim.

Things to do

If you are interested in insects and would like to know more about them, there are lots of places you can write to for information. Here are a few useful addresses:

The British Entomological and Natural History Society
Dinton Pastures Country Park
Davis Street
Hurst
READING
Berkshire
RG10 0TH

This society studies all sorts of British insects.

The British Dragonfly Society
68 Outwoods Road
LOUGHBOROUGH
Leicestershire
LE11 3LY

This society has local groups around Britain. It also organises field trips to watch dragonflies and damselflies.

The British Butterfly Conservation Society
PO Box 222
Dedham
COLCHESTER
Essex
CO7 6EY

A society which organises the study and conservation of butterfly habitats.

World Wide Fund for Nature (WWF)
Panda House
Weyside Park
GODALMING
Surrey
GU7 1XR

The WWF is trying to save endangered animals, including insects, all over the world.

Glossary

abdomen The third part, or tail end, of an insect's body. It holds the insect's heart and is where the insect digests its food. A female insect has a tube at the tip of her abdomen for laying eggs.

antennae The "feelers" on an insect's head. They are used for smelling and for testing how fast the wind is blowing.

compound Made up of many different parts. An insect has compound eyes which are made up of many different lenses.

hive A man-made home for bees. People keep bees in hives so that they can collect the honey made by the bees.

larva A caterpillar or a grub. When the eggs of most insects hatch, a larva comes out. It looks totally different to the adult insect of the same kind.

lenses The parts of the eye which help it to see in focus.

nectar A sweet, syrupy liquid that is made by flowers to attract insects to them.

pollen A yellow dust-like powder that is made by the male parts of flowers. If some pollen lands on the female part of a flower, a seed may grow which will become a new plant.

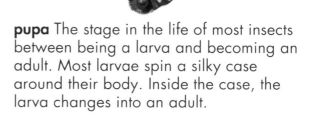

pupa The stage in the life of most insects between being a larva and becoming an adult. Most larvae spin a silky case around their body. Inside the case, the larva changes into an adult.

sap The juice which flows around the inside of a plant. It carries the plant's food and water supplies.

thorax The second, or middle, part of an insect's body. An insect's wings and legs are attached to its thorax.

31

Index

Photographic credits:
Bruce Coleman Ltd (J Cancalosi) 13,
(C Hughes) 7, (K Rushby) 29,
(K Taylor) 25, (P Ward) 16,
(K Wothe) 4; NHPA (ANT/D & T
O'Byrne) 9, (S Dalton) 3, 19,
22, 26, (S Krasemann) 21,
(I Polunin) 10, (J Shaw) 15.